Debby Ryan

by **Sarah Tieck**

Big Buddy Books
An Imprint of Abdo Publishing
www.abdopublishing.com

www.abdopublishing.com

Published by Abdo Publishing, a division of ABDO, PO Box 398166, Minneapolis, Minnesota 55439.
Copyright © 2015 by Abdo Consulting Group, Inc. International copyrights reserved in all countries. No part
of this book may be reproduced in any form without written permission from the publisher. Big Buddy Books™
is a trademark and logo of Abdo Publishing.

Printed in the United States of America, North Mankato, Minnesota.
092014
012015

THIS BOOK CONTAINS
RECYCLED MATERIALS

Cover Photo: Jordan Strauss/Invision/AP.
Interior Photos: ASSOCIATED PRESS (pp. 11, 13); Hubert Boesl/picture-alliance/dpa/AP Images (p. 15); Disney
    Channel via Getty Images (pp. 17, 23, 27); Getty Images (pp. 7, 9, 21, 29); John Shearer/Invision/AP (p. 24);
    Todd Williamson/Invision/AP (p. 5); WireImage (pp. 17, 19).

Coordinating Series Editor: Rochelle Baltzer
Contributing Editors: Bridget O'Brien, Marcia Zappa
Graphic Design: Maria Hosley

Library of Congress Cataloging-in-Publication Data

Tieck, Sarah, 1976-
  Debby Ryan : Disney TV star / Sarah Tieck.
    pages cm. -- (Big buddy biographies)
  ISBN 978-1-62403-572-2
1. Ryan, Debby, 1993---Juvenile literature. 2. Actors--United States--Biography--Juvenile literature. 3. Singers-
-United States--Biography--Juvenile literature. I. Title.
  PN2287.R865T54 2015
  791.4502'8092--dc23
  [B]
                          2014026439

Debby
Ryan

Contents

Rising Star

Debby Ryan is an actress and singer. She also plays music, writes songs, and helps make albums. She has appeared in television shows and movies. Debby is known for starring in *Jessie* and *The Suite Life on Deck*.

Tennessee

• Huntsville

Alabama

Mississippi

Georgia

Florida

GULF OF MEXICO

Family Ties

Deborah Ann "Debby" Ryan was born in Huntsville, Alabama, on May 13, 1993. Her parents are Missy and John Ryan. Her older brother is Chase.

Debby and Chase are both talented musicians.

Growing Up

Debby's dad was in the military. For a time, her family lived in Germany. Debby began acting in theater shows on the American military base there.

In 2003, the family moved to Texas. There, Debby continued acting. She also **performed** as her school **mascot**.

Debby's early performances helped her prepare for life as an actress.

Lights! Camera! Action!

Debby knew she wanted to be an actress. So, she tried out for **professional** acting parts. In 2007, Debby got a part in *Barney: Let's Go to the Firehouse*. She also had small parts in other movies, television shows, and **commercials**.

Barney is a singing, dancing purple dinosaur. He stars in videos and a children's television series.

Making It Big

In 2008, Debby got a main part in *The Suite Life on Deck*. She played Bailey Pickett. Bailey is a country girl who wants to see the world. She dates Cody Martin, who is played by Cole Sprouse.

In 2010, Debby starred in *16 Wishes*. This Disney television movie became very popular. It is about a girl who gets 16 wishes on her 16th birthday. About 5.6 million people watched its premiere!

Debby, Dylan Sprouse, Brenda
Song, Cole Sprouse, and Phill Lewis
(*left to right*) made up the main cast
of *The Suite Life on Deck*.

A Star Is Born

The Suite Life on Deck came to an end in 2011. But that year, Debby got her biggest **role** yet. She began starring in the television show Jessie! This was an important step in her acting **career**.

Debby plays Jessie Prescott, a small-town girl who moves to the city. She was excited to have a lead role!

In 2014, Jessie got engaged. Jessie will be the first main character on a Disney show to get married.

Debby has had many opportunities to build her career on *Jessie*. She helped come up with the idea for the show. And in 2014, she directed an episode.

Jessie

Jessie is a popular show on the Disney Channel. On the show, Jessie moves from Texas to New York City, New York.

She wants to become an actress. But instead, she takes a job as a nanny for four children. The show follows her adventures in the city.

In 2014, Michelle Obama appeared on *Jessie*. The episode was about military families.

Debby acts with (*from left to right*) Karan Brar, Skai Jackson, Peyton List, and Cameron Boyce. They play the kids Jessie nannies.

New Opportunities

Debby's **role** on *Jessie* made more people notice her talent. Soon, Debby had more chances to act. She got parts in television shows including *Private Practice* and *The Glades*. And she starred in a television movie called *Radio Rebel*.

Debby enjoyed working with the cast of *Radio Rebel* (*above*). The movie is about a shy high school girl with a secret.

Music Lover

Aside from acting, Debby loves music. She is a singer, songwriter, musician, and record **producer**. Debby often works with her brother on new music. And, she is part of a band called the Never Ending. In 2014, they **released** an **EP** called *One*.

In 2010, Debby performed during the Disney Parks Christmas Day Parade.

An Actress's Life

As an actress, Debby is very busy. She must practice lines for her **roles**. During filming, she works on a **set** for several hours each day.

As a singer and songwriter, Debby writes and records songs. Sometimes she practices **performing** them.

In 2012, Debby was the host of *Make Your Mark: The Ultimate Dance Off - Shake It Up Edition.*

23

Many people take Debby's picture at events.

Debby's talents as an actress and a singer have made her popular. She has many fans! Debby appears in magazines and attends events. She also talks to reporters for news stories.

Off the Screen

Debby spends free time with her family. She likes to read books. She also enjoys hanging out with friends, watching movies, and eating s'mores.

Debby likes to help others. She is a Disney Friends for Change Ambassador. In 2012, she traveled to India to help build a school.

In 2014, Debby read to children at the White House Easter Egg Roll.

27

Buzz

Debby's opportunities continue to grow. Debby wants to start a record label that helps recording artists grow creatively. She also wants to continue to broaden her acting **career**.

Fans are excited to see what is next for Debby Ryan. Many believe she has a bright **future**!

Snapshot

★**Name**: Deborah Ann "Debby" Ryan

★**Birthday**: May 13, 1993

★**Birthplace**: Huntsville, Alabama

★**Appearances**: *Barney: Let's Go to the Firehouse, The Suite Life on Deck, 16 Wishes, Jessie, Private Practice, The Glades, Radio Rebel*

★**EP**: *One*

Important Words

career work a person does to earn money for living.

commercial (kuh-MUHR-shuhl) a short message on television or radio that helps sell a product.

EP extended play. A music recording with more than one song, but fewer than a full album.

future (FYOO-chuhr) a time that has not yet occurred.

mascot something to bring good luck and help cheer on a team.

perform to do something in front of an audience.

premiere (prih-MIHR) the first time a play, film, or television show is shown.

producer a person who oversees the making of a movie, a play, an album, or a radio or television show.

professional (pruh-FEHSH-nuhl) working for money rather than only for pleasure.

release to make available to the public.

role a part an actor plays.

set the place where a movie or a television show is recorded.

Websites

To learn more about Big Buddy Biographies, visit **booklinks.abdopublishing.com**. These links are routinely monitored and updated to provide the most current information available.

Index